getting a grip series

GW00360502

setting up and running
mid-week clubs for children

not just
Sunday

Margaret Withers

The National Society
*Leading Education
with a Christian Purpose*
Church House Publishing

National Society/Church House Publishing
Church House
Great Smith Street
London SW1P 3NZ

ISBN 0 7151 4982 2

Published 2002 by National Society Enterprises Ltd

Tel: 020 7898 1557
Fax: 020 7898 1449
Email: copyright@c-of-e.org.uk

Cover design by Church House Publishing
Typeset in Helvetica light 9pt
Printed in England by Halstan & Co. Ltd,
Amersham, Bucks

Contents

Foreword

For many years, churches have been looking for ways to expand their children's work beyond the traditional pattern of activities in the church hall on Sundays. With a growing appreciation of the Church's role in the community throughout the week, there are increasing opportunities to meet children within their environment and culture and to help them to discover the gospel in the way that is appropriate for them.

My Officer for Evangelism among Children, Margaret Withers, was appointed to help the Church to focus on the ways that it can effectively communicate the gospel to children and serve the needs of the community to which they belong. She has written this small book to help churches take practical steps towards reaching children in the community through a number of midweek activities.

I am delighted to commend this very useful contribution and hope that many churches will apply its suggestions.

+ George Cantuar

The Most Revd and Rt Hon Dr George Carey
Archbishop of Canterbury

1   Aims and objectives

Introduction

Children's work is often thought of as being something that happens on Sunday. That has been the pattern for over 200 years. During that time, and especially in the last 30 years, society has altered beyond recognition. A child's life is changing rapidly. The Church needs to respond to this by reaching children where they are, respecting their culture and their vulnerability.

Jesus' main ministry was in the streets and the countryside. He met people where they were and served their needs. We should do the same. The Church is the people of God, being Christ in the community. You are doing that already by thinking about working with children in some way during the week.

First steps

The purpose of this book is to take you through the first steps of planning and setting up midweek children's activities. It helps you to research your project, then gives advice about involving your church, your local authority and the people who will be working with you. It gives general information about legal matters, funding and training, but, as each organization is different, you will need to get detailed information about this from your diocesan office and your local authority. You may also want to seek help from organizations connected with children's clubs.

Section 7, 'Running a session' (p. 17) gives advice on organization, the Christian content, and tips on resources and outside help. It is beyond the scope of this small book to suggest the content of the programme or reflect on the subject of children's spirituality. Several books on this are listed in Section 12, 'Further help' (p. 30).

Much of the information is given in lists. Do not be daunted by them. Work through each one, ticking off the things that you are doing already. You will probably find that most of the requirements demand little or no work.

Usual types of club

Let us start by looking at some of the children's clubs that are operating, the reasons for starting them, and what we hope will be the results.

Pre-school and toddler clubs meet regularly in church halls. Some of them are run by the church, and other groups are there as tenants. In both cases, they provide opportunities for contact with the parents and youngsters.

After school clubs have operated in the community for a decade. Some of them are latchkey provision, held in schools or libraries; others are run by churches and other voluntary organizations. The number of clubs is growing, but demand far outstrips supply. An increasing number of churches see such a club as a major form of outreach.

Common types of children's clubs

Age in years	0	1	2	3	4	5	6	7	8	9	10	11	12	13	14	+
Daily				Pre-school ---												
Weekly	Toddler club ----------															
Weekly	Crèche during services --															
Weekly						Uniformed organizations ----------------------------------->										
Weekly						After school club ------------------										
Weekly									Christian Union in school ----------------->							
Weekly												Junior Youth group -->				
Monthly	Pram service ---------															
Monthly	Young parents' worship ----															
As required				Services geared towards children ---												
As required						Fun morning ----------------------										
As required						Holiday club -----------------------										
As required												Youth worship -------->				
Age in years	0	1	2	3	4	5	6	7	8	9	10	11	12	13	14	+

Informal midweek worship designed for a children's or youth group is becoming popular. This will include teaching and other activities within the framework of the service.

Saturday morning clubs are usually held once a month or as single events. Some of them are geared towards a special service on the following day; others provide a safe environment while parents are shopping.

A fun morning or holiday club is the simplest activity. Some are geared towards a Family Service on the next Sunday; others contain basic Christian teaching, designed for children with little knowledge of the Christian faith.

Uniformed organizations do valuable work with children and young people. They have their own structures so they are not discussed here. Links with the church need to be valued and encouraged.

What are our reasons for starting a club?

Your answers will probably include a social aspect and an evangelistic focus. Here are some suggested answers:

1. Sunday has become a day for visits to grandparents, and second parents in cases of split families. Shopping, sports and schools activities are increasingly taking place on Sunday. A midweek club could provide Christian nurture and worship that cater especially for children who cannot come on Sunday.

2. In areas of deprivation with inadequate housing, an after school club could provide a safe environment, with games and teaching, for children who would otherwise have nowhere to go.

3. Parents with young families will welcome a couple of hours when their children can enjoy activities at little or no cost to the family budget. Furthermore, many parents do not finish work until after school ends so an after school club could provide valuable support.

4. The demand for wraparound care through breakfast and after school clubs is increasing rapidly. Church schools and churches can be in the forefront of this provision. Very few parishes could provide a daily club on their own but could allow their premises to be used by the local authority or a Christian organization like the YMCA.

5. Parents and carers of young children often feel isolated and would welcome a toddler club. This could be a form of outreach to post-baptismal families, and might include Christian songs and prayer within the other activities.

6. Some churches have few facilities and the main services do not cater for children. A midweek club with activities and a short service allows children or young people to explore the gospel and worship God in a style that is appropriate for their age and culture.

7. Holiday clubs are valuable forms of outreach. Similar activities during Holy Week, at half-term, or on some Saturday mornings could increase the contact and opportunities for Christian teaching. They could also be linked to a Family Service on the next Sunday.

What are our aims?

They may include:

*   Witnessing to the gospel through working with children in the community.
*   Providing a service to the local community.
*   Supporting young parents, especially those who suffer deprivation.
*   Giving children accessible ways of discovering the gospel.
*   Encouraging more children and parents to come to church.

What do we expect to happen?

*   Children will have an opportunity to discover the gospel and worship God in a way that is appropriate for their age and culture.
*   Children's innate spirituality will be given a chance to grow, in a Christian context.
*   For many young parents, the worship in the toddler club or pram service will be their experience of 'Church'. It will give their babies an experience of worship from a very early age. It will also give parents an opportunity to ask questions and discuss matters concerning their lives and faith.
*   Some children may make an initial contact with the church through a Family Service. We must accept, however, that few of them will attend

church frequently. Increasing the congregation should not be the primary aim of starting any children's club.

● Some of the children may come to Christian commitment later, or come to church to be married or have their children baptized.

Take some time to think about your aims for your club.

Looking ahead
The journey to faith is a long one. We live in an age that demands instant results. It is hardly surprising, therefore, that children's workers can get dispirited. We are sowing seeds of faith, however, and we can trust that, in God's own time, there will be a harvest.

2   Researching the project

Before presenting any ideas to a Church Council or starting initial planning, you need to decide what sort of club is needed and what facilities you will need to provide for its successful operation. You may have found a clear need already, but it is always worth researching around the request to check its viability.

In the community
Think or discuss:

- What are the needs of the children in our parish and wider community?
- What are the needs and resources of their families?
- What facilities and clubs are operating already?

Ask questions in your local community: your neighbours, schools, health centre and library as well as at your church. Discover what activities and clubs for children already exist. Note any clubs that were started but not successful. This may be because the original plans were flawed, but it could mean that there was not as much demand as had been perceived. The replies will help you to decide what kind of club is needed and what resources you require.

Always seek to cooperate with and complement other organizations. Look for a free afternoon and a missing activity rather than competing with other clubs and activities.

Having decided where there is a need, ask if you are responding to it in the best way. For example, an after school club might be run more effectively in the school than the church hall, if all of the children are pupils there.

Places and people
Think or discuss:

- Do we have a venue that is suitable and accessible?
- Do we have people to lead, coordinate or help?

The kind of club you run depends on the numbers of leaders available, the size of the premises and the standard of the facilities. The Children Act and Health and Safety legislation have contributed to ensuring that our children's activities take place in safe and well-maintained premises with adequate numbers of adults present.

Venues
The church hall or parish room is the most obvious choice of venue. Advantages are space, cheapness and ease of forming links with other church-based activities. Halls are rarely used during the late afternoons. Some activities or worship can include visiting the church building. Furniture or equipment can be shared with other church activities. Possible disadvantages are safety standards, suitability for young children

and distance from the children's homes and schools. If your church is considering refurbishing or developing its hall or room, see that plans include provision for young children as well as adults.

Schools are designed for children and have resources ranging from play space to suitable furniture. In some communities, most of the children will attend the same school so the problem of transporting them does not arise. Disadvantages are that you may have to pay rent for the premises and will have to remove all equipment at the end of each session. However, it could be a valuable way for the parish and its school to work together.

Church buildings are underused. Most modern churches adapt easily for a variety of activities. The disadvantages of using ancient buildings for children's clubs are obvious, but, with good heating and lighting, plus some imagination, quite a lot can be achieved. A children's corner would make a suitable venue for a small toddler group. If the church has chairs, they can be moved to create an open space. The churchyard is a wonderful area for nature trails and treasure hunts. The advantage is that the children become familiar with the church building and will be at ease if they visit it for a main service.

Private houses are possible for small numbers of children or for toddler groups. Ideally, they should not have more than ten people in them and are more appropriate for nurture groups than an open club. Extra care has to be taken with child protection issues in an informal setting.

In the community. Churches have run children's clubs in rooms over pubs, libraries, and doctors' surgeries. A few are starting in supermarkets while parents do the shopping. They will all have basic facilities and may even be free of charge. Being there will witness to the community and reach people who would normally not attend a church service.

Personnel

Many churches select their children's workers with great care. Others are grateful to accept anyone who volunteers. Basic criteria for all people who work with children are given in Section 6, 'Leaders and helpers' (p. 15) and should always be followed.

It is usually better to seek out and invite people to help with children's work than to wait for volunteers. Some people do not realize that they have the skills required, so do not put themselves forward; others are reluctant to volunteer because they wonder if they can cope with a band of lively youngsters. They can gain experience by helping an experienced leader on a fun day or holiday club before making a commitment. Youngsters aged less than 18 years are often valuable and capable helpers but should not work without an adult present.

All adult staff should sign a Criminal Disclosure form before starting working with children. If you are planning a weekly club for quite a large number of children, consider paying a trained person to lead it. This will guarantee continuity and standards. Details about this are given in Section 6, 'Leaders and helpers' (p. 15).

3 Involving your church

The Church Council

Now that you have done your basic research, the next step is to take your plans to the Parochial Church Council. The incumbent and PCC are ultimately responsible for all work undertaken in the name of their church. This includes the safety and well-being of the children in any club or activity. You will need their permission to start the club, as well their prayerful support.

It is sensible and courteous to have an informal talk with your vicar or minister before going to the meeting. Try to write down as much information as is possible and think through any likely questions. Make it clear from the outset what financial and other support you hope the PCC will provide.

The PCC must approve all leaders and helpers in the club. If leaders and helpers have not done children's work in your church before, they should offer references and sign Criminal Disclosure forms. Further information on this is given in Section 5, 'Legality and good practice' (p. 12) and Section 6, 'Leaders and helpers' (p. 15).

Most churches are happy to support a children's club financially as part of their evangelism programme. If you are using the church hall, you may be required to pay a nominal rent. This will depend on how popular the hall is and whether you are charging for membership.

The congregation

Let the congregation know about your plans. Ask for its prayers and use people's expertise. This can range from legal advice to designing flyers. You may identify potential leaders from the congregation or parents in the local school. When the club has started, ask the congregation to provide scrap for craft activities. This way, everyone can be involved.

Raising the profile

Most children's clubs are held midweek and during the day, so the congregation does not see them in action. It is vital that the parish should own this work as part of its mission among children.

1. Make the club accountable by asking the PCC for a budget, however small.
2. Report on the club at the AGM and PCC meetings.
3. Write regularly in your parish magazine to keep the congregation informed.
4. Ask the clergy to include the club regularly in the parish prayers and the notices.
5. Invite individuals to undertake to pray regularly for the club. This is a good way of keeping housebound people involved in the life of the church.

6.   Ask the clergy to find ways of affirming the work. This could include commissioning of new leaders.

7.   Invite the clergy and PCC to spend a session with you.

8.   Ask people with particular skills or hobbies to help with a specific activity.

9.   Make attractive displays of children's activities or work and put them in the church.

10. Invite the children to services like Christingle and Mothering Sunday. Involve some children in them if possible.

4 The local authority

The next step is to consider what advice you need from your local authority and other professional bodies.

Read on!

The temptation is to say that this is a Church group so does not need to bother with 'red tape'. Recent legislation, especially the Children Act (1989), has improved standards of childcare, and, if we value our children, we will want to ensure their well-being. Local authorities are usually delighted when churches start clubs for children, as they do not have the resources to meet the demand themselves.

There are six reasons for informing your local authority that you are planning to start a children's club:

1. Viability

You have researched your project very carefully and have decided that your club is needed. There may be, however, information that you do not know. For example:

- Another church may have had the same idea and already made plans.
- You think that your parish needs a pre-school but there may be vacancies in other pre-schools in the area.
- The local authority may want to start an after school club in your area. This could be a chance to work together.

2. Serving the community

You may feel that your club will be very small so that the above information will not apply to you. It is still worth making your plans known so that social workers and health visitors can pass the information on to families who would benefit from it. For example:

- Many parents and carers are lonely and would enjoy the company of a toddler group.
- An after school club could provide safe childcare for a youngster whose parent is ill or working late. Some local authorities will pay for places for children in need.
- Holiday clubs and play schemes allow children to meet their friends and play in a safe environment. You could receive a grant to support your work.

3. Registration

This is the process of checking that the leader is suitable to care for children in safe and suitable premises. It involves an annual inspection. OFSTED has recently taken over registration from the local authorities. Registration normally costs £14.00 and is obligatory if:

- the children are aged under eight years;
- the club runs for two or more hours a day on six or more days a year;
- the purpose of the club is care based, rather than providing a specific activity. Groups like church choirs or football clubs will probably be exempt from registration.

To register a club, contact your local Early Years' Officer. They have application packs and will provide any help that you need. Clubs for children aged from eight years do not need to be registered. It is proposed that OFSTED will provide 'Certificates of suitability' for these groups some time after 2003.

Clubs that run for under two hours, or for five or less days a year are exempt from registration provided OFSTED is notified in writing. This will normally involve telephoning the Regional Centre and completing a simple form for its records. Regional Centres may be contacted by calling the general OFSTED helpline on 0845 601 4771.

4. Health and safety

In addition to an OFSTED inspection, the Early Years' Officer wll give advice on premises, numbers, and health and safety matters. The official will advise on the number of children that can be accommodated, basic provision such as toilet facilities, and possible safety hazards like a kitchen or main road.

In most cases, the officers are positive and helpful. Occasionally, a leader will feel that his or her demands are unrealistic. If this is the case, ask whether you are being asked to comply with a ruling or a suggestion. For example, it is obligatory to have washing facilities with the toilets, but only desirable to have liquid soap.

5. Early Years Development and Childcare

The government has developed a programme of care for children aged between four and fourteen years. This is run by the Department for Education and Skills (DfES). Each local authority is required to form a partnership of organizations and interested parties to deliver the programme. Aspects in which the church is involved include Under Fives, Pre-schools, and Out of School care.

The Early Years' Development Officer will provide you with a great deal of advice and, in certain circumstances, you can receive funding and training.

6. Children's Information Service

The CIS is a new initiative sponsored by the DfES. It provides a central point of contact covering all aspects of childcare within a local authority. The main function is to provide accurate and impartial information on childminders, nurseries, pre-schools, and out of school activities. It also has information on support for groups, including toy libraries, funding and training opportunities.

If your club is registered, it will go on the CIS register. This will give you valuable publicity and opportunities to reach families who are seeking help. The information provided is useful to group leaders. The usual means of access is via a dedicated phone line.

Where to go next

Your diocesan children's adviser will be able to give you a certain amount of advice. Contact him or her through your diocesan office or website.

Each Early Years Development and Childcare Partnership has places for Church representatives. Your diocesan representative may be the children's adviser or have been nominated by the Board of Education or Church in Society. Contact your diocesan office to find out who this is. He or she will be able to give you local advice as well as names of people to contact.

Local authority departments are listed in the telephone book and website. Look under either Early Years, or Childcare. OFSTED's helpline is 0845 601 4771. Advice can also be found through it's website, www.ofsted.gov.uk.

5 Legality and good practice

Children are valuable. They are also vulnerable, so their care and nurture should be one of the most important parts of our ministry.

When we are working with children, we are *in loco parentis*, taking the place of parents. This is too big a responsibility to rely on good will and chance. We cannot know a group of youngsters as well as parents know their children, so we need simple procedures to help us. Work through the following checklists. You will probably find that you can tick off many of the items already. They are for general guidance. When in doubt, always seek clarification.

A. Legal matters

1. The legal responsibility rests with the PCC. Its permission needs to be obtained for any church activity.

2. Inform the insurers. Starting a children's club will not affect your premium unless it involves sporting or residential activities, but the company should be consulted.

3. Every parish should have a child protection policy based on diocesan guidelines. This includes requiring people who work with children to sign a Criminal Disclosure form. If you need advice, contact your diocesan office and ask to speak to the Child Protection Officer.

4. Social Services give advice on legal, and health and safety matters. You may need to register the club with OFSTED. Information on this is given in Section 4, 'The local authority' (p. 10).

B. Health and safety

1. All publicity and information should give the name of your church, the club, and its venue.

2. Information should include the name of the leader and a contact address.

3. Premises should fulfil Health and Safety standards. Leaders should have a written procedure for evacuating the building quickly or getting help in emergency.

4. Have a properly stocked first aid kit with one assigned person, preferably trained, to take charge of first aid. All accidents and administration of medicines should be fully recorded.

5. Know where the nearest telephone is if you do not have a mobile phone.

6. Do not let children go home without an adult unless the parent has said that they may do so. Never let a child go with another adult unless the parent has informed you that this will be happening.

7. Have some simple safety rules such as staying in places, lining up for drinks, asking before going to the toilet, standing still when the whistle blows. This will lower the risk of accidents and improve the quality of the activities.

C. Membership

When a child joins the club, ask the parents to fill in a registration form. This should include:

- Name;
- Home address and phone number;
- Date of birth;
- Two names and contact phone numbers in case of emergency;
- Basic medical information including the name and address of the child's GP.
- It is helpful to invite information about learning difficulties, fears, and family situations like a recent death or an absent parent.

D. Daily operation

1. Keep a register. This may be crucial in case of emergency or of a child not turning up. It should remain on the premises.
2. A minimum adult ratio of 1:8 is recommended for children aged eight or more years. There should be more adults if the children are younger or for group outings.
3. Gear the programme to the numbers of adults present, the premises and facilities.

E. Outings

1. If you have an outing, see that the parents have full details of the activity and sign a consent form. Take the consent forms with you.
2. If you use private cars, inform the parents of the names of the drivers. Check the drivers' insurance and licences. Never overload a car or travel in one that does not have rear seatbelts.
3. You need to display a permit if you take a group of children in a minibus. The DVLA has an information leaflet on the use of minibuses. Contact 01792 782318 or the website, www.open.gov.uk/dvla/
4. Check with the church's insurance company that you are covered for activities that take place away from the church premises.

F. Cause for concern

1. Should a child turn up without their parents' knowledge or without a registration form, you should try to contact the home immediately. Such cases are rare and usually arise from thoughtlessness.

2. Once a child comes into the club, you have taken responsibility for him or her. This is preferable to leaving a small child alone in the street. Try to discover any medical conditions or allergies. Do not give any food or allow him or her to join in lively games in case of accident.

3. When the child's parent or carer does appear, speak to him or her in private. Explain why it is in everyone's interests that you know about the child and the whereabouts of a responsible adult. Taking a firm but not punitive line will usually resolve the situation.

4. Should any child not have been collected by the time you have cleared up after the end of the session, contact the parent or emergency contact numbers.

5. If you have to take a child away from the premises, for example, because the hall is being locked, see that you inform the parent or leave a clear written message. Take the child to a safe place nearby, preferably with more than one adult present.

6. If you are concerned about a child's welfare for any reason, follow the directions given in your Child Protection Policy. Should you need advice, contact the diocesan child protection officer, the local Social Services, or the NSPCC helpline on 0808 800 5000. Never ignore concerns, however small they may seem.

6 Leaders and helpers

The success of your club will depend largely upon the quality of your leaders and their helpers. The local authorities have the following criteria for people working with children. They are based on the Home Office Document, *Safe from Harm*.

1. Previous experience of looking after or working with children. If there is no such experience, the leader should be willing to undertake training during the first twelve months.

2. The ability to provide warm and consistent care.

3. A willingness to respect the background and culture of all children in their care.

4. A commitment to treat all children as individuals and with equal concern.

5. Reasonable physical health, mental stability, integrity and flexibility.

Think or discuss how you will apply these criteria to a Christian club.

Training and experience
- Check whether your leaders and helpers have experience of working with children.

- As part of affirming the importance of the work, the PCC should encourage and pay for leaders and helpers to have some training. Further information is given in Section 8 on 'Training' (p. 19).

- If appropriate, consider employing a qualified and paid leader to lead the club and help to train the other staff.

Valuing our children
- The criteria describing the attitude of the leaders towards the children in their care embody sound Christian principles of recognizing each child as a unique being, made in the image of God.

- Discuss what basic rules are needed to ensure that we treat the children fairly and consistently.

- Children's cultural backgrounds and situations will be wide ranging. They may include minority ethnic and religious groups, maybe with English being the second language. The children will come from a variety of families. Some will have parents who work away from home, on shifts, or who are unemployed. Discuss ways of being sensitive to the children's cultural backgrounds and individual needs.

Affirming our leaders and helpers
- Children's workers need to have reasonable physical and mental health, and to be able to cope with the unexpected or stressful situation.

- They set an example of the way that the children should behave so they need to be open and honest, with respect for other people and the community. Children will learn how Christians behave from their example.

- Christian teaching must respect the children's culture and vulnerability, and be without coercion or manipulation.

Support and evaluation

- Any work that you do for your church is the legal responsibility of the PCC. It has delegated the work to you. To demonstrate this, the PCC should endorse the appointment of all children's leaders and helpers. This states that the church considers the leaders to be appropriate people to work with children and will give them its support. Keep the PCC informed about the club. Be prepared to raise any concerns and ask for support with addressing any difficulties.

- Child protection procedures protect and support children's workers as well as children. Each diocese has its child protection guidelines. These stipulate that all new leaders should sign a Criminal Disclosure form and give names of two referees. If a person is unwilling to sign such a form or you are uneasy about their suitability, do not use them. It is better to risk offending an adult than harming a child.

- Have regular meetings to plan and evaluate work. This is even more important for a small group as more responsibility falls on each individual. Be prepared to discuss problems openly within the group and to praise or constructively criticize each other. Use books, videos and training sessions to keep your work imaginative and up to date.

- Children's workers, like everyone else, need time off for illness, holidays, or personal reasons. It is advisable to have two or three people who will help in emergency. These may be former children's workers, parents, or someone from another children's group. Knowing that help is at hand does a great deal to avoid stress among workers and problems among the children.

7 Running a session

Guiding principles

The length and content of a session depends on the aims, age, and background of the children, the number of staff, and the venue and resources. The content is not discussed in detail here, but there are various programmes and schemes available. Some of them are listed at the end of this book.

The style of activities and level of Christian witness or teaching will depend on the children and the nature of the club. An after school club in the village school will have a different ambience from one on an urban housing estate. A toddler club operating as part of community outreach will be different from one that comprises post-baptismal families.

Age range

Some clubs have clear rulings about the age of the children. Pre-schools operate for children aged two years and nine months, to five years. Uniformed organizations have age-related sections. Decide what age range and number of children you will have in your club and plan the sessions accordingly.

Timing

If the club is meeting immediately after school, have drinks and biscuits available as the children arrive. Always take a register.

End each session with a quiet exercise such as reading a story, a 'goodbye' song or a prayer. This will encourage the children to leave the premises calmly and happily. Allow time for clearing up, especially after craft or games with equipment.

Resources

Take advice before buying resources or equipment. Talk to other group leaders. Some local education authorities allow voluntary children's clubs to use their resources centres. This will allow you to buy goods at a greatly reduced rate. Staff should be available to advise you on what is suitable for your group.

Avoid buying large equipment unless you will use it regularly and have adequate storage space. Some councils will lend large toys and equipment, sometimes for a small fee.

Some dioceses and youth organizations have resources centres and will lend videos, and small equipment like badge-making machines and parachutes for group games.

Christian content

Make it clear on your publicity if your sessions will include simple Christian teaching or visits to the church. Respect children from other faiths and cultures.

Any Christian teaching or worship must be appropriate for the age and understanding of the children. You cannot assume that the children will have any knowledge of the

Christian faith, the Bible, or prayer. Plan this part of the session very carefully. Sit the children around a carpet or in a circle as this helps them to be calm. Lighting a candle, and simple directions like the traditional, 'hands together, eyes closed' for the prayer time are helpful. Seek to give the children an awareness of the presence of God and his love for each one of them. Never exclude a child from worship for bad behaviour or suggest that he or she is not valuable to God for any reason.

People living in the Middle East, thousands of years ago, wrote the Bible. It can seen very remote to children living in western Europe in the twenty-first century. If you include Bible stories in your session, see that you use an attractive version that is suitable for the children's age range. Relate it to the children's lives by setting the scene or with a few questions and answers. Always remember that you are telling the story of God's loving relationship with his people. This relationship continues today.

Charities
Charities are always willing to give presentations or talks about their work. Many of them have speakers who are trained to work with children. Christian Aid, CMS, and Mission to Seafarers provide excellent educational packs and teaching materials. A special charity each term or year gives a focus on the outside world. Older children enjoy fund-raising activities like sponsored walks or sleepovers. Any child can contribute to simple activities like creating a mile of pennies or making cakes or cards to sell.

Special events
Have an outside speaker or someone to teach a new skill to the group each term. Activities like pottery or cooking are popular. Outings, Christmas parties, Easter egg hunts, and other celebrations all add to the sense of celebration and community within the group. Be sensitive to family circumstances and provide help with costs if necessary.

Other specialist help and advice
Kid's Club Network provides advice, training and various publications, including: *School's Out, Guidelines for Good Practice for Out of School Care Schemes.*

Pre-School Learning Alliance (PLA) is an umbrella organization linking pre-schools and supporting the active involvement of parents. It provides training and publications.

Pre-School Playgroups Association aims to enhance the development of pre-school children. It publishes information, training sheets and guidelines.

Rural Sunrise specializes in work with small and rural churches. The children's coordinator advises on strategic planning, fun days, holiday and after school clubs. It has a set of excellent biblically based resources.

Scripture Union runs Christian clubs in schools and the wider community. It has local field workers and will provide training, advice and resources.

Their addresses are given at the end of the book.

8 Training

Nationally recognized qualifications

Local colleges offer full-time and part-time courses in subjects like Childcare and Education, Early Childhood Studies, and Playwork. They range from NVQ levels 2 and 3, to diplomas and advanced diplomas. There are both full-time and part-time courses. Modules can be selected to focus on the student's particular interests. Much of the work is practical and is assessed at the student's place of work. Contact your local FE College for information.

Local authorities often offer free training for people who are working in registered children's clubs. This usually consists of an Advanced Certificate in Playwork, which provides the basis for an NVQ level 3, and courses like first aid, and child protection. It is always worth enquiring about training, even if your club is not registered. The local authority may take any children's workers if the course is not fully subscribed. The Early Years' Officer will have details.

Training and advice

Registered groups with children aged under eight years require 50 per cent of the staff to have an NVQ level 3 or a similar qualification. The course is largely practical. It is held at a FE college with visits to your place of work.

It is worth being trained, even if it is not required. It will give you a greater understanding of and interest in the work. A nationally recognized qualification would be useful should you decide to make children's work your career or want to work for another organization.

Uniformed organizations

Uniformed organizations have their own training programmes. They include subjects like first aid and child protection.

Christian organizations

A few colleges and organizations like Children World Wide, Scripture Union and CPAS offer courses. They range from extended training to one day events. Your diocesan children's adviser should provide training and general advice. Courses include 'Kaleidoscope' (NCEC), and 'Fired Up!' (BRF) or you may request specific training. The availability and standard of training varies according to the area and annual programme.

9 Money matters

The question of money appears in every project. Even the smallest groups need to decide about paying for premises, providing resources, drinks and biscuits.

Planning a budget

Think or discuss:

- Can we get financial help from anywhere?
- Are there any organizations to help us?
- What support will the parish be able to give?
- Where do we find resources and advice on activities and equipment?
- How much, if anything, should we charge for attending the club?

Charities

This is a vast source of money and advice. Seek help from people in your diocese who will know about local funds. Some parishes and districts have charities that were originally set up to provide education for children. Look at:

- The Church Urban Fund
- Children's charities
- Local Church charities
- Diocesan Mission charities.

Local authority funding

Contact the Early Years' Officer to inquire about financial help. Social Services will often pay for places for children from needy families. Local Partnerships will give grants for new work or extending existing work with after school projects. This comes for the government's New Opportunities Fund. Inquire about making a bid when you discuss your plans with your local Early Years' officer.

In rural areas, contact the Parish Council, District Council and the regional Countryside Agency (Vital Villages project). They often give grants for holiday clubs and may support ongoing projects.

Business sponsorship

Small businesses and shops may help by funding specific items in exchange for publicity. They may provide resources at a reduced price or free of charge. Even if the sums are small, it is part of generating goodwill between the Church and the community. Most large local businesses like factories or airports have a policy of providing funds for local projects.

Sources of funding and resources

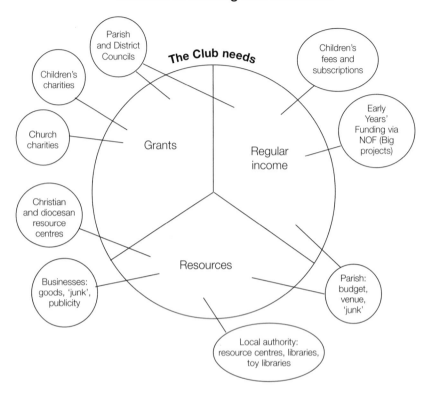

Parish support

The club is part of the parish's outreach in the community. The PCC should include some financial support in its budget. It could allow you to use premises rent-free or for a low rent that covers costs. Sharing equipment and collecting junk for craft activities help to cut costs.

Resources

Look for cheaper options before buying in high street stores. Education authorities have resource centres that provide equipment for schools at a vastly reduced rate. Enquire whether you can become a member. Cash and carry stores are excellent value for food and small equipment. It is worth hiring equipment that you only use occasionally or is difficult to store. Advice on resources is given in Section 7, 'Running a session' (p. 17).

Staff costs

Most church clubs are small and are run by volunteers. Be prepared, however, to cover some costs. Have a fund for training and books connected with the work. The leaders may see the work as part of their Christian stewardship but, if they are retired or on limited incomes, they will appreciate being offered travel expenses.

You may wish to offer an honorarium to a leader as part of a contract. Large clubs often have paid staff. It is vital that a Christian organization should be a fair and honest employer. If the PCC is not used to employing staff, take professional advice.

Membership fees

A small charge for a membership card guarantees a regular income and is a way of monitoring membership numbers. In cases of hardship, it is easy to give cards without a charge or to offer membership at a reduced rate for large families.

After school clubs in schools and pre-schools currently charge about £3.00 a session. In some deprived areas, it would be counterproductive to ask for payment for the club.

Any decisions concerning membership fees must be considered carefully in light of other local practices and family need.

10 Schools, a valuable resource

Goodwill

Given that a school is a community where representatives of several hundred people of all ages and backgrounds meet under one roof, it is worthwhile forging links with the local schools.

Your contact with a school will depend entirely on the goodwill of the headteacher and Board of Governors. Many community or private schools welcome visitors from the local worshipping communities. Some become governors. Others help with RE lessons and acts of worship or run a Christian club during the lunch hour. Some headteachers, however, do not wish to forge such links for a variety of reasons.

Church schools are in the forefront of mission. A good Church school is a Christian beacon in the community. The relationship between the parish and its school can be a vital and rewarding one. This depends on the attitude of the headteacher and Board of Governors as well as the church.

Basic information

Entry to any school is by the headteacher's invitation. That includes governors, parents and clergy as much as other visitors. You will need the headteacher's permission to distribute publicity or information about activities or clubs. Seek permission in plenty of time and send a copy of the flyer or letter to the headteacher in advance. Most Church schools and some other schools are willing to distribute publicity about Church activities.

If the headteacher is unwilling for you to be involved, it may be for good reasons. Spend time forming relationships rather than making demands.

Using the premises and equipment

Schools are ideal places for holiday or midweek clubs Rent is usually reasonable. If you plan to hold a holiday club, see that you book it well in advance. You cannot guarantee that the school will be available as major cleaning, repairs, and building work always take place in the holidays.

Always remember that you are guests and rely on goodwill. Leave the premises tidy and orderly. It is very depressing for a teacher to arrive on the following morning to find the classroom disrupted or pictures and displays damaged.

Never use school equipment without permission. It is stealing to use the school's paper, pens or coffee. Purchasing resources through the school skews its budget and may involve VAT fraud so should not be done.

Types of club

Apart from holiday clubs and fun days, other ways of working with the children in the school are:

- Latchkey or homework club;
- After school activities with Christian teaching;
- Christian Union.

Pre-school activities

Some churches run an independent pre-school in a spare classroom in the local school. This has the advantage of providing suitable premises and use of equipment. The children may become involved in school activities like acts of worship and the end of term celebrations. When they move into the main school, the building and many of the people will be familiar.

Bear in mind that rent must cover all of the costs of servicing and maintaining the classroom. It would be an improper use of school funds to subsidize the pre-school by charging only a nominal rent. Should the school roll increase, the pre-school would have to vacate the classroom for the new children. See that there is adequate notice on either side and have a contingency plan ready when you see that this is a possibility.

Parents, carers and toddlers

Parents, other carers and toddlers congregate in or near the school playground every afternoon. If there is an afternoon when the hall or a room is vacant, consider holding a toddler club there.

It may be possible to reach young families by running an occasional pram service in the school hall. Many parents will attend a simple service if it is in familiar surroundings, but would not feel at ease in a church.

11　Case studies

Church-led children's clubs fall under five basic headings:

A.　Toddler groups.

B.　Pre-schools and nurseries.

C.　Midweek clubs that are based on worship and teaching.

D.　Clubs that are led by non-church leaders but retain strong links with the church.

E.　Holiday clubs and fun days.

Here is an example of each type of club. None of them is a perfect model because they are real situations. Only their names have been altered.

A. A parent and toddler club in a village

Crickwich is a village of 1,000 people, with few amenities. The small congregation is elderly. Four years ago, the new vicar arrived to find several families wanting to have their babies baptized. He realized that the mothers needed a chance to meet each other and socialize. From these families, he and his wife started a toddler group. Each session included a Christian song and a prayer.

After a couple of years, two mothers said they wanted to come to church but felt that they could not cope with their toddlers in the service. This led to a weekday informal service followed by activities for the children and seekers' discussion for adults. This group is small but makes up 22 per cent of the worshipping congregation. The toddlers occasionally take part in a special Sunday service. One mother has started to attend the church regularly on Sunday and is showing signs of potential leadership.

B. A Church-led pre-school in a suburb

Buckleigh is a wealthy suburban parish. Judy started her own pre-school in the church hall twelve years ago. It has been taken over by the PCC who appointed a sub-committee to manage it. It has just passed its OFSTED inspection. It describes itself as a Christian pre-school but welcomes children of all faiths and none. Teaching includes Bible stories and prayers, visiting the church to see the Christmas crib and Easter garden, and an annual service. Judy and two of the assistants are members of the congregation. The vicar visits it frequently. He knows all the children and many of the parents.

The pre-school has led to an increase in goodwill between local young families and the church. Several families are bringing babies for baptism or asking the vicar for pastoral or spiritual advice. Some parents are taking the children into church to look around and say a prayer. The Crib service on Christmas Eve is 'standing room only'.

C. An after school club based on worship and teaching

Borton is a deprived inner-city area. Three 'Kidz Klubs', based on the work of Bill Wilson in New York, operate every Thursday in term time. The venue is the church building. The chairs are assembled to face a small platform from which the action takes place. Leaders and helpers are identified by special T-shirts. They greet the children by name. The children file into their seats and wait for the action to start. The style is slapstick with lots of shouting and cheering of the teams.

After the welcome, the rules are sung: 'Stay in your seat, obey your team captain, the whistle means silence'. A leader guides a child in the opening prayer, followed by songs. Then come a couple of games. One of them links to the following teaching. The other one is a team game to sort out a Scripture text. This is followed by another song, then a teaching slot.

The session ends with another song and prayer and a collection for this term's charity. About 400 children come each week to one of three sessions. Each pair of leaders has a group of children assigned to them. They visit each child every Tuesday to deliver a colouring sheet and be available to chat.

D. Partnership in a multicultural urban area

When Peter became vicar of St Paul's Northaven, he found that the biggest need in the area was for activities for children and young parents. He approached the Social Services and suggested that they work together to turn the church hall into a community centre and start children's clubs.

- The church provided the original hall, a large room with a stage and a kitchen.
- Funding from Social Services, the Church Urban Fund and a diocesan charity paid to convert it into two rooms with modern kitchen and toilet facilities.
- The YMCA runs the activities. The staff is paid out of the government's New Opportunities Fund.

The division of the hall into two rooms allowed the present tenants, the uniformed organizations, to stay while other groups grew alongside them. The YMCA runs a carer and toddler club, pre-school, after school club, and a playscheme throughout each holiday. Each group has 'St Paul's' in its title. Other clubs for young people include dancing and judo classes.

Over 300 children come to St Paul's Community Centre each week. Every child knows the parish priest. He is a valued visitor in the schools. Eighty children attended an All Saints' service. The centre and its activities have put the church back where it belongs, in the middle of the community. The parish is proud of the project and describes it as, 'sowing seeds through service'. It has allowed the after school and holiday clubs to have the premises rent-free for three years. Rent for other groups is negotiated according to need.

E. A Fun Morning in a village within the London commuter belt

Upperhill has 45 children living in the village. In most cases, both parents are at work, and many of the children are cared for by au pairs. The Sunday School closed down ten years ago. The churchwardens decided to hold an activity morning on the day before Mothering Sunday to link with a special family service. Every child received a personal invitation and 30 turned up. Activities included a treasure hunt in the church and making banners and cards for the next morning. There were 18 children with their parents at the Sunday service.

Three years later, the parish holds a fun morning every quarter before a special service. A monthly family service is established. Several young families attend it. The church plans to hold its first holiday club next year.

Using the models

Your proposed club will probably not be exactly like any of these. We can learn from each example and use the information in our own planning. You may think that a club's programme or its relationship with the church could be developed further. Some aspects you may want to alter.

Vision. Each of these clubs started through the vision of one person. He or she saw a need and addressed it. You may be the person with a vision for the children in your community.

Pastoral care. The secret of success lies in the level of pastoral care and personal contact. In each case the children are known and valued. They know and are at ease with the clergy and leaders.

Appropriate. Each club is an example of being the Church in the community. It engages with the children where they are, in every sense. The two midweek clubs, C and D, are both responding to social deprivation in different ways. The level of Christian witness and teaching is that which is appropriate for the situation.

Worship. In three examples, A, C and E, the groups are breaking the mould to create forms of worship that suit their situations and stages of faith. This worship needs to be owned and recorded by the parish. Other projects have led to increased baptisms and attendance at special services.

Service. The parishes with the pre-school and the community centre, B and D, see their aim as being to serve the community. This is part of our Christian witness and should not be underestimated. One priest commented, 'You serve first. Jesus did not say, "I will only love you after you have followed me".'

Slow but sure. In each case, the organizers planned their project carefully and developed the work slowly. An initial burst of enthusiasm can lead to trying to do too much at once. It inevitably ends with bankruptcy or burnout.

Children's clubs: linking the church and community

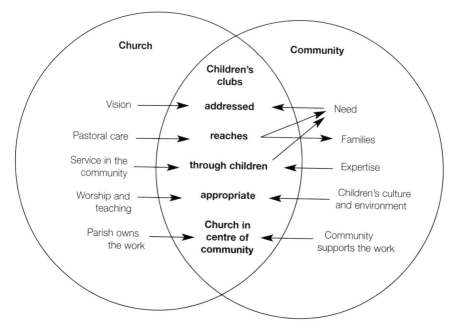

Recognition. Some of the leaders claimed that their difficulty lay in getting the congregation to own the work as part of its mission among children, although it supported it financially. Parish D, however, saw the work in the community centre as being part of its mission and was very proud of it. Teaching on ways of being Church, regular prayer, reports and visits are vital to keep the work in the mind and heart of the parish.

Hallmarks of success
Think or discuss:

- Is there anything that we can learn from these examples?
- How can we apply each of the above factors to our proposed children's work?
- Is there anything that we want to change in our planning?

12 Further help

Christian organizations

Bible Reading Fellowship (BRF)
First Floor, Elsfield Hall
15–17 Elsfield Way
Oxford, OX2 8FG
Tel: 01865 319700
email: info@brf.org.uk
website: www.brf.org.uk

'Barnabas', the children's section of BRF, provides contributions to children's events, and biblically based resources for children and their leaders. 'Barnabas Live' brings the Bible alive for primary-aged children by using the creative arts.

Church Pastoral Aid Society (CPAS)
Athena Drive
Tachbrook Park
Warwick, CV34 6NG

Tel: 01926 334242
email: mail@cpas.org.uk
website: www.cpas.org.uk

The major Anglican evangelistic organization. Its many activities include training, advice, courses and camps. Its numerous resources include the all-age project *Under Construction*.

CURBS
PO Box 344
Redhill
Surrey, RH1 3FG

Tel: 01737 642522
email: curbs.project@virgin.net
website: www.curbs.freeserve.co.uk

CURBS (Children in URBan Situations) was set up to produce Christian resources geared to the needs of children in inner cities and on outer urban estates. It has produced a number of activity packs known as 'CURBStone Kits'. It provides advice, networking and a vision for children's work, set in the context of ongoing support and training of leaders.

Rural Sunrise
2 The Old Forge
Gardner Street
Herstmonceux
Hailsham
East Sussex, BN27 4LE

Tel: 01323 832083
email: rural.missions@zetnet.co.uk

This is part of Sunrise Ministries, which specializes in work with small and rural churches. It advises on strategic planning, fun days, holiday and after school clubs. It also has resources, including midweek club programmes.

Scripture Union
207–209 Queensway
Bletchley
Milton Keynes
Bucks. MK2 2EB

Tel: 01908 856000
email: info@scriptureunion.org.uk

A major non-denominational evangelistic organization. Provides training, hands-on work, and resources. Its publications include a large number for use with children.

Specialist children's organizations

Kid's Club Network
279–281 Whitechapel Road
London, E1 1BY

Tel: 020 7247 3009
website: www.kidsclubs.co.uk

PCCA Christian Child Care
PO Box 133
Swanley
Kent, BR8 7UQ

Tel: 01322 667207
Help line: 01322 660011
email: info@pcca.co.uk

Pre-School Learning Alliance (PLA)
69 Kings Cross Road
London, WC1X 9LL

Tel: 020 7833 0991
website: www.pre-school.org.uk

Pre-School Playgroups Association
61–63 Kings Cross Road
London, WC1X 9LL

Tel: 020 7833 0991

Publications

Handbooks
Bell, David and Heathfield, Rachel, *Mission Possible*, Scripture Union/CPAS, 2000.

Bridger, Francis, *Children finding Faith*, Scripture Union/CPAS, 1986.

Butler, Paul, *Reaching Children*, Scripture Union, 1993.

Frank, Penny, *Bringing Children to Faith*, Scripture Union/CPAS, 2000.

Frank, Penny, *Children and Evangelism*, CPAS, 1992.

Frank, Penny, *Every Child – a Chance to Choose*, Kingsway/CPAS, 2002.

Pritchard, Gretchen Wolff, *Offering the Gospel to Children*, Cowley, 1992.

Safe From Harm, HMSO, 1994.

Holiday clubs

Ambrose, Gill and Bond, Ruth, *Plagues and Promises*, National Christian Education Council, 1998.

Charters, Alan and Hardwick, John, *The Ultimate Holiday Club Guide*, BRF, 1994.

Fountain, Ron, *Go for Gold*, (book and video), Scripture Union, 2000.

Godfrey, Paul, *MegaQuest*, Scripture Union, 2001.

Wallis, Paul, *Desert Diary* (book and video), Scripture Union, 2001.

Leaders' training

Frank, Penny, *Leading Children*, CPAS, 1998.

Withers, Margaret, *Fired up . . . not burnt out*, BRF, 2001.

Kaleidoscope, (Revised edition), National Christian Education Council, 1998.

Midweek clubs and projects

Bruce, Elizabeth and Jarvis, Judy, *The Paintbox Project*, National Christian Education Council, 2000.

Clark, Philip and Pearson, Geoff, *Kidz Klubs: the Alpha of Children's Evangelism?*, Grove Books, 1999.

Gibb, Claire, *Building New Bridges*, National Society/Church House Publishing, 1996.

Griffiths, Mark, *Fusion*, Monarch, 2001.

Murrie, Diana and Pearce, Steve, *All Aboard*, National Christian Education Council, 1996.

Stephenson, John, *The Story Keepers* (book and video), Scripture Union, 1997.

Under fives

Farley, Jane, Goddard, Eileen and Jarvis, Judy, *Under Fives – Alive!*, National Society/Church House Publishing, 1997.

Farley, Jane, Goddard, Eileen and Jarvis, Judy, *Under Fives – Alive and Kicking!*, National Society/Church House Publishing, 1999.

Godfrey, Jan, *Praise, Play and Paint!*, National Society/Church House Publishing, 1995.

Howie, Vicki, *Easy Ways to Bible Fun for the Very Young,* BRF, 2001.

Worship and spirituality

Ambrose, Gill, *The 'E' Book*, National Society/Church House Publishing, 2000.

Astley, Jeff, *How Faith Grows*, National Society/Church House Publishing, 1991.

Box, Su, *The Lion Book of First Prayers*, Lion, 1998.

Fuller, Jill, *Looking Beyond*, Kevin Mayhew, 1996.

Herbert, Christopher, *Prayers for Children*, National Society/Church House Publishing, 1995.

Stone, Mary K., *Don't Just Do Something – Sit There*, RMEP, 1995.

COMMON WORSHIP RESOURCES FOR KIDS!

My Communion Book – A Child's Guide to Holy Communion

£4.50   0 7151 4946 6 *(Single copy)*
£22.00   0 7151 4977 6 *(Pack of 6)*

Diana Murrie s book takes the child through the service of Holy Communion. Designed to complement *Common Worship*, this bright, engaging book is ideal for any parent or children s worker seeking to help children understand and enjoy the Holy Communion service. Full colour throughout — great illustrations.

The Communion Cube

£4.95   0 7151 4976 8

Aimed at slightly younger children, this robust cube introduces the child to the communion service in a fun and simple way. Perfect for stimulating children in those quieter moments at church.

Come and Join the Celebration
A resource book to help adults and children experience Holy Communion together

John Muir and Betty Pedley
£12.95   ISBN 0 7151 4947 4

Since the introduction of *Common Worship*, churches everywhere are thinking afresh about their worship — especially about Holy Communion. This offers a perfect opportunity for parishes to think further about how to include children in their Eucharist worship.

The National Society
*Leading Education
with a Christian Purpose*
Church House Publishing

Available from all good Christian bookshops or direct from Church House Bookshop on 020 7898 1300 or order securely online: www.chbookshop.co.uk